CONTENTS
Tunes included in VOLUME 129 are:

D1709222

Song Title	Track #	Song Title	Track #
1. Frosty The Snowman	1	9. We Wish You A Merry Christmas	9
2. Here Comes Santa Claus	2	10. Home For The Holidays	10
3. Up On The Housetop	3	11. Jingle Bells	11
4. Jingle Bell Rock	4	12. Angels From The Realms Of Glory	12
5. Over The River & Through The Woods	5	13. Snowfall	13
6. Angels We Have Heard On High	6	14. Jolly Old St. Nick	14
7. All I Want For Christmas Is My Two Front Teeth	7	---- Jolly Old St. Nick (Shuffle)	15
8. There's A Song In The Air	8	---- Tuning Notes (Bb & A Concert)	16

Lyrics...ii

𝄞 CONCERT KEY SONGS & CHORD SCALE/PROGRESSIONS...........................1

𝄙 Bb INSTRUMENT SONGS & CHORD SCALE/PROGRESSIONS.....................17

𝄙 Eb INSTRUMENT SONGS & CHORD SCALE/PROGRESSIONS.....................33

𝄢 BASS CLEF INSTRUMENT SONGS & CHORD SCALE/PROGRESSIONS.....49

Complete Play-A-Long Listing...65

Any codas (⊕) that appear will be played only once
on the recording at the end of the <u>last</u> recorded chorus.

PLAY-A-LONG CD INFORMATION
STEREO SEPARATION: LEFT CHANNEL = Bass & Drums; RIGHT CHANNEL = Piano & Drums
TUNING NOTES: Concert Bb & A (A=440)

PERSONNEL ON PLAY-A-LONG RECORDING
STEVE ALLEE - Piano; TYRONE WHEELER - Bass; JONATHAN HIGGINS - Drums

Published by
JAMEY AEBERSOLD JAZZ®
P.O. Box 1244
New Albany, IN 47151-1244
www.jazzbooks.com
ISBN 978-1-56224-279-4

Engraving
MIKE HYZIAK

Cover Design
JASON A. LINDSEY

BOOK ONLY: $5.95 U.S.

LYRICS

1. FROSTY THE SNOW MAN

Frosty the snowman was a jolly happy soul,
With a corncob pipe and a button nose and two eyes made out of coal.
Frosty the snowman is a fairy tale, they say,
He was made of snow but the children know how he came to life one day.
There must have been some magic in that old silk hat they found.
For when they placed it on his head he began to dance around.
O, Frosty the snowman was alive as he could be,
And the children say he could laugh and play just the same as you and me.
Thumpetty thump thump, Thumpety thump thump, look at Frosty go.
Thumpetty thump thump, Thumpety thump thump, over the hills of snow.

Frosty the snowman knew the sun was hot that day,
So he said, "Let's run and we'll have some fun now before I melt away."
Down to the village, with a broomstick in his hand,
Running here and there all around the square saying, catch me if you can.
He led them down the streets of town right to the traffic cop.
And he only paused a moment when he heard him holler "Stop!"
For Frosty the snow man had to hurry on his way,
But he waved goodbye saying, "Don't you cry, I'll be back again some day."
Thumpetty thump thump, Thumpety thump thump, look at Frosty go.
Thumpetty thump thump, Thumpety thump thump, over the hills of snow.

2. HERE COMES SANTA CLAUS

Here comes Santa Claus! Here comes Santa Claus!
Right down Santa Claus Lane!
Vixen and Blitzen and all his reindeer are pulling on the reins.
Bells are ringing, children singing; All is merry and bright.
Hang your stockings and say your prayers,
'Cause Santa Claus comes tonight.

Here comes Santa Claus! Here comes Santa Claus!
Right down Santa Claus Lane!
He's got a bag that is filled with toys for the boys and girls again.
Hear those sleigh bells jingle jangle, what a beautiful sight.
Jump in bed, cover up your head,
'Cause Santa Claus comes tonight.

3. UP ON THE HOUSETOP

Up on the housetop reindeer pause, out jumps good old Santa Claus
Down thru the chimney with lots of toys all for the little ones,
Christmas joys

Ho, ho, ho! Who wouldn't go? Ho, ho, ho! Who wouldn't go?
Up on the housetop, click, click, click,
Down thru the chimney with good Saint Nick

First comes the stocking of little Nell, Oh, dear Santa fill it well
Give her a dolly that laughs and cries, one that will open and shut her eyes

Ho, ho, ho! Who wouldn't go? Ho, ho, ho! Who wouldn't go?
Upon on the housetop, click, click, click
Down thru the chimney with good Saint Nick

Look in the stocking of little Will, Oh, just see what a glorious fill!
Here is a hammer and lots of tacks, whistle and ball and a whip that cracks

Ho, ho, ho! Who wouldn't go? Ho, ho, ho! Who wouldn't go?
Up on the housetop, click, click, click
Down thru the chimney with good Saint Nick

4. JINGLE-BELL ROCK

Jingle bell, jingle bell, jingle bell rock, Jingle bells swing and jingle bells ring
Snowing and blowing up bushels of fun, now the jingle hop has begun

Jingle bell, jingle bell, jingle bell rock, Jingle bells chime in jingle bell time
Dancing and prancing in Jingle Bell Square, in the frosty air.

What a bright time, it's the right time to rock the night away
Jingle bell time is a swell time to go gliding in a one-horse sleigh

Giddy-up jingle horse, pick up your feet, jingle around the clock
Mix and a-mingle in the jingling feet
That's the jingle bell, that's the jingle bell, that's the jingle bell rock.

5. OVER THE RIVER AND THROUGH THE WOODS

Over the river and through the woods to Grandmother's house we go.
The horse knows the way to carry the sleigh
Through white and drifted snow.

Over the river and through the woods, oh, how the wind does blow.
It stings the toes and bites the nose as over the ground we go.

Over the river and through the woods to have a full day of play.
Oh, hear the bells ringing ting-a-ling-ling, for it is Christmas Day.

Over the river and through the woods, trot fast my dapple gray;
Spring o'er the ground just like a hound, for this is Christmas Day.

Over the river and through the woods
And straight through the barnyard gate.
It seems that we go so dreadfully slow; It is so hard to wait.

Over the river and through the woods, now Grandma's cap I spy.
Hurrah for fun; the pudding's done; Hurrah for the pumpkin pie.

6. ANGELS WE HAVE HEARD ON HIGH

Angels we have heard on high, singing sweetly through the night,
And the mountains in reply echoing their brave delight.
Gloria in excelsis Deo. Gloria in excelsis Deo.

Shepherds, why this jubilee? Why these songs of happy cheer?
What great brightness did you see? What glad tiding did you hear?
Gloria in excelsis Deo. Gloria in excelsis Deo.

Come to Bethlehem and see him whose birth the angels sing;
Come, adore on bended knee Christ, the Lord, the new-born King.
Gloria in excelsis Deo. Gloria in excelsis Deo.

See him in a manger laid whom the angels praise above;
Mary, Joseph, lend your aid, while we raise our hearts in love.
Gloria in excelsis Deo. Gloria in excelsis Deo.

7. ALL I WANT FOR CHRISTMAS IS MY TWO FRONT TEETH

Every body stops and stares at me
These two teeth are gone as you can see
I don't know just who to blame for this catastrophe!
But my one wish on Christmas Eve is as plain as it can be!

All I want for Christmas is my two front teeth,
my two front teeth, see my two front teeth!
Gee, if I could only have my two front teeth,
then I could with you "Merry Christmas."
It seems so long since I could say, "Sister Susie sitting on a thistle!"

Gosh oh gee, how happy I'd be, if I could only whistle.
All I want for Christmas is my two front teeth,
my two front teeth, see my two front teeth.
Gee, if I could only have my two front teeth,
then I could wish you "Merry Christmas!"

LYRICS (cont.)

8. THERE'S A SONG IN THE AIR
There's a song in the air! There's a star in the sky!
There's a mother's deep prayer and a baby's low cry!
while the beautiful sing, for the manger of Bethlehem cradles a King!

There's a tumult of joy o'er the wonderful birth,
for the virgin's sweet boy is the Lord of the earth.
Ay! the star rains its fire while the beautiful sing,
for the manger of Bethlehem cradles a King!

In the light of that star lie the ages impearled;
and that song from afar has swept over the world.
Every hearth is aflame, and the beautiful sing
in the homes of the nations that Jesus is King!

We rejoice in the light, and we echo the song
that comes down through the night from the heavenly throng.
Ay! we shout to the lovely evangel they bring,
and we greet in his cradle our Savior and King!

9. WE WISH YOU A MERRY CHRISTMAS
We wish you a merry Christmas, we wish you a merry Christmas
We wish you a merry Christmas and a happy New Year.
Glad tidings we bring to you and your kin;
Glad tidings for Christmas and a happy New Year!

We want some figgy pudding, we want some figgy pudding
We want some figgy pudding please bring it right here!
Glad tidings we bring to you and your kin;
Glad tidings for Christmas and a happy New Year!

We won't go until we get some ,we won't go until we get some
We won't go until we get some so bring it out here!
Glad tidings we bring to you and your kin;
Glad tidings for Christmas and a happy New Year!

We wish you a Merry Christmas, we wish you a Merry Christmas
We wish you a Merry Christmas and a happy New Year.
Glad tidings we bring to you and your kin;
Glad tidings for Christmas and a happy New Year!

10. HOME FOR THE HOLIDAYS
Oh, there's no place like home for the holidays,
'Cause no matter how far away you roam
When you pine for the sunshine of a friendly face
For the holidays, you can't beat home, sweet home

I met a man who lives in Tennessee and he was headin' for Pennsylvania
And some home made pumpkin pie
From Pennsylvania folks a travelin' down to Dixie's sunny shore
From Atlantic to Pacific, gee the traffic is terrific

Oh there's no place like home for the holidays,
'Cause no matter how far away you roam
If you want to be happy in a million ways
For the holidays, you can't beat home, sweet home

11. JINGLE BELLS
Dashing through the snow, in a one-horse open sleigh
Over the fields we go, laughing all the way;
Bells on bob-tail ring, making spirits bright
What fun it is to ride and sing a sleighing song tonight

Jingle bells, jingle bells, jingle all the way!
O what fun it is to ride in a one-horse open sleigh
Jingle bells, jingle bells, jingle all the way!
O what fun it is to ride in a one-horse open sleigh

A day or two ago, I thought I'd take a ride
And soon Miss Fanny Bright, was seated by my side;
The horse was lean and lank, misfortune seemed his lot;

He got into a drifted bank and we got upsot

Jingle bells, jingle bells, jingle all the way!
O what fun it is to ride in a one-horse open sleigh
Jingle bells, jingle bells, jingle all the way!
O what fun it is to ride in a one-horse open sleigh

A day or two ago, the story I must tell
I went out on the snow, and on my back I fell;
A gent was riding by, in a one-horse open sleigh
He laughed as there I sprawling lie but quickly drove away
Jingle bells, jingle bells, jingle all the way!
O what fun it is to ride in a one-horse open sleigh
Jingle bells, jingle bells, jingle all the way!
O what fun it is to ride in a one-horse open sleigh

Now the ground is white, go it while you're young
Take the girls tonight, and sing this sleighing song;
Just get a bob-tailed bay, two-forty as his speed
Hitch him to an open sleigh and crack! you'll take the lead

Jingle bells, jingle bells, jingle all the way!
O what fun it is to ride in a one-horse open sleigh
Jingle bells, jingle bells, jingle all the way!
O what fun it is to ride in a one-horse open sleigh

12. ANGELS FROM THE REALMS OF GLORY
Angels, from the realms of glory, Wing your flight o'er all the earth;
Ye, who sang creation's story, Now proclaim Messiah's birth:
Come and worship, Come and worship
Worship Christ, the new-born King.
Shepherds in the field abiding,Watching o'er your flocks by night,
God with man is now residing; Yonder shines the infant Light:
Sages, leave your contemplations, Brighter visions beam afar:
Seek the great Desire of nations; Ye have seen his natal star:
Saints before the altar bending, Watching long in hope and fear,
Suddenly the Lord, descending, In his temple shall appear.

13. SNOWFALL
Snowfall, snowfall, glistening snowfall
Snowflakes Falling, winter calling

Frozen lays, everyplace down they come
Twirling, tumbling lightly, brightly, lovely snowfall

Lightly, brightly, lovely snowfall, lovely snowfall

14. JOLLY OLD ST. NICK
Jolly old Saint Nicholas, lean your ear this way!
Don't you tell a single soul what I'm going to say;
Christmas Eve is coming soon; Now, you dear old man,
Whisper what you'll bring to me; Tell me if you can.

When the clock is striking twelve, when I'm fast asleep,
Down the chimney broad and black, with your pack you'll creep;
All the stockings you will find hanging in a row;
Mine will be the shortest one, you'll be sure to know.

Johnny wants a pair of skates; Susy wants a dolly;
Nellie wants a story book; She thinks dolls are folly;
As for me, my little brain isn't very bright;
Choose for me, old Santa Claus, what you think is right.

iii

1. Frosty The Snow Man

PLAY 4 CHORUSES (♩ = 120)

Words and Music by Steve Nelson and Jack Rollins

1

1. Frosty The Snow Man – Cont.

2. Here Comes Santa Claus

(Right Down Santa Claus Lane)

PLAY 5 CHORUSES (♩ = 192) FORM: AAB

Words and by Music by
Gene Autry and Oakley Haldeman

Repeat and fade out

3. Up On The Housetop

PLAY 7 CHORUSES (♩ = 126)

Words and Music by Benjamin Hanby

4. Jingle-Bell Rock

PLAY 4 CHORUSES ($\bullet$ = 144)

Words and Music by Joe Beal and Jim Boothe

5. Over The River
And Through The Woods

PLAY 7 CHORUSES (♩ = 166)

Play two times and end at Fine 2nd time

Fine

6. Angels We Have Heard On High

PLAY 6 CHORUSES (♩ = 120)

Traditional French Carol/James Chadwick

7. All I Want For Christmas Is My Two Front Teeth

PLAY 5 CHORUSES (♩ = 130)

Words and Music
by Don Gardner

8. There's A Song In The Air

PLAY 5 CHORUSES (♩ = 126) FORM: ABABC

Words and Music by Josiah G. Holland
and Karl P. Harrington

Play 3 times   ritard.

9. We Wish You A Merry Christmas

PLAY 4 CHORUSES (♩ = 132) FORM: ABABC

Traditional

10. Home For The Holidays

PLAY 5 CHORUSES (♩ = 192)

Lyrics by Al Stillman
Music by Robert Allen

10. Home For The Holidays – Cont.

11. Jingle Bells

PLAY 6 CHORUSES (♩ = 200)

Words and Music by James Pierpont

12. Angels From The Realms of Glory

PLAY 4 CHORUSES (♩ = 120) FORM: ABABC

Words by James Montgomery
Music by Henry Smart

13. Snowfall

Music by Claude Thornhill, Lyrics by Ruth Thornhill

14. Jolly Old St. Nicholas

16

1. Frosty The Snow Man

PLAY 4 CHORUSES (♩ = 120)

Words and Music by Steve Nelson
and Jack Rollins

17

1. Frosty The Snow Man – Cont.

2. Here Comes Santa Claus

(Right Down Santa Claus Lane)

PLAY 5 CHORUSES (♩ = 192) FORM: AAB

Words and by Music by
Gene Autry and Oakley Haldeman

19

3. Up On The Housetop

PLAY 7 CHORUSES (♩ = 126)

Words and Music by Benjamin Hanby

4. Jingle-Bell Rock

5. Over The River
And Through The Woods

Traditional

SOLOS

CODA

Play two times and end at Fine 2nd time   *Fine*

6. Angels We Have Heard On High

PLAY 6 CHORUSES (♩ = 120)

Traditional French Carol/James Chadwick

Fine

7. All I Want For Christmas Is My Two Front Teeth

PLAY 5 CHORUSES (♩ = 130)

Words and Music
by Don Gardner

9. We Wish You A Merry Christmas

PLAY 4 CHORUSES (♩ = 132)   FORM: ABABC

Traditional

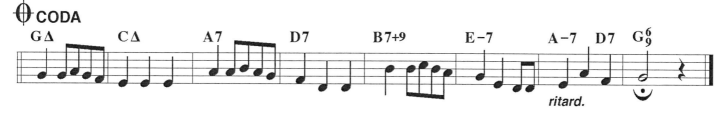

ritard.

(There's No Place Like)
10. Home For The Holidays

PLAY 5 CHORUSES (♩ = 192)

Lyrics by Al Stillman
Music by Robert Allen

Copyright © 1957 Roncom Music Co.
Copyright Renewed 1982 assigned to Charlie Deitcher Productions, Inc.
All Rights Reserved   International Copyright Secured   Used by Permission

27

10. Home For The Holidays – Cont.

11. Jingle Bells

12. Angels From The Realms of Glory

PLAY 4 CHORUSES (♩ = 120) FORM: ABABC

Words by James Montgomery
Music by Henry Smart

14. Jolly Old St. Nicholas

PLAY 9 CHORUSES [TRACK #14]
PLAY 7 CHORUSES [TRACK #15 *Shuffle version*]

Traditional

1. Frosty The Snow Man

PLAY 4 CHORUSES (♩ = 120)

Words and Music by Steve Nelson
and Jack Rollins

33

1. Frosty The Snow Man – Cont.

2. Here Comes Santa Claus
(Right Down Santa Claus Lane)

Words and by Music by
Gene Autry and Oakley Haldeman

3. Up On The Housetop

Words and Music by Benjamin Hanby

PLAY 7 CHORUSES ($\quad = 126$)

36

4. Jingle-Bell Rock

PLAY 4 CHORUSES (♩ = 144)

Words and Music by Joe Beal and Jim Boothe

5. Over The River
And Through The Woods

PLAY 7 CHORUSES (♩ = 166)

Traditional

Play two times and end at Fine 2nd time

6. Angels We Have Heard On High

PLAY 6 CHORUSES ($\quad$ = 120)

Traditional French Carol/James Chadwick

Fine

7. All I Want For Christmas Is My Two Front Teeth

Words and Music
by Don Gardner

PLAY 5 CHORUSES (♩ = 130)

8. There's A Song In The Air

PLAY 5 CHORUSES (♩= 126) FORM: ABABC

Words and Music by Josiah G. Holland
and Karl P. Harrington

9. We Wish You A Merry Christmas

PLAY 4 CHORUSES (♩ = 132) FORM: ABABC

Traditional

(There's No Place Like)
10. Home For The Holidays

PLAY 5 CHORUSES (♩= 192)

Lyrics by Al Stillman
Music by Robert Allen

10. Home For The Holidays – Cont.

44

11. Jingle Bells

PLAY 6 CHORUSES (♩ = 200)

Words and Music by James Pierpont

45

12. Angels From The Realms of Glory

PLAY 4 CHORUSES (♩ = 120) | FORM: ABABC

Words by James Montgomery
Music by Henry Smart

Repeat and fade out

13. Snowfall

Music by Claude Thornhill, Lyrics by Ruth Thornhill

47

14. Jolly Old St. Nicholas

Traditional

PLAY 9 CHORUSES [TRACK #14]
PLAY 7 CHORUSES [TRACK #15 *Shuffle version***]**

1. Frosty The Snow Man

PLAY 4 CHORUSES (♩ = 120)

Words and Music by Steve Nelson
and Jack Rollins

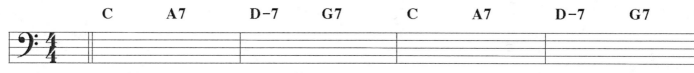

2. Here Comes Santa Claus
(Right Down Santa Claus Lane)

PLAY 5 CHORUSES (♩ = 192) FORM: AAB

Words and by Music by
Gene Autry and Oakley Haldeman

Repeat and fade out

51

3. Up On The Housetop

PLAY 7 CHORUSES ($\bullet$ = 126)

Words and Music by Benjamin Hanby

4. Jingle-Bell Rock

PLAY 4 CHORUSES (♩ = 144)

Words and Music by Joe Beal and Jim Boothe

5. Over The River
And Through The Woods

PLAY 7 CHORUSES (♩ = 166)

Traditional

Play two times and end at Fine 2nd time

Fine

6. Angels We Have Heard On High

PLAY 6 CHORUSES (♩ = 120)

Traditional French Carol/James Chadwick

Fine

7. All I Want For Christmas Is My Two Front Teeth

PLAY 5 CHORUSES ($\bullet$ = 130)

Words and Music
by Don Gardner

8. There's A Song In The Air

PLAY 5 CHORUSES (♩= 126) | FORM: ABABC

Words and Music by Josiah G. Holland
and Karl P. Harrington

Play 3 times   *ritard.*

9. We Wish You A Merry Christmas

PLAY 4 CHORUSES (♩ = 132) | **FORM: ABABC**

Traditional

ritard.

(There's No Place Like)

10. Home For The Holidays

Lyrics by Al Stillman
Music by Robert Allen

PLAY 5 CHORUSES (♩ = 192)

59

10. Home For The Holidays – Cont.

SOLOS

D | CΔ | FΔ | CΔ | D-7 G7 | CΔ | A7

D7 A♭7 G7 | | CΔ C7 | FΔ F♯°7 | CΔ | CΔ E♭°7

E-7 A7 | D-7 G7 | CΔ | C7 | **E** FΔ | ⟋

FΔ F♯° | C/G C♯° | D-7 | G7 | CΔ | C7

FΔ | ⟋ | FΔ F♯° | C/G C-6 | B-7 E7 | A-7 D7

G7 C♯° | D-7 G7 | **F** CΔ | FΔ | CΔ | D-7 G7

CΔ | A7 | D7 | G7 | CΔ C7 | FΔ F♯°7

CΔ | CΔ E♭°7 | E-7 A7 | D-7 G7 | C | D-7/G ⊕

⊕ **CODA**

CΔ | D-7/G | CΔ | D-7/G | CΔ | D-7/G   *Repeat and fade out*

BOSSA

60

11. Jingle Bells

PLAY 6 CHORUSES (♩ = 200)

Words and Music by James Pierpont

12. Angels From The Realms of Glory

PLAY 4 CHORUSES (♩ = 120) FORM: ABABC

Words by James Montgomery
Music by Henry Smart

13. Snowfall